IL PENSEROSO

BY

JOHN MILTON

AND

WILLIAM BLAKE

MELANCHOLY AND HER COMPANIONS

JOHN MILTON

IL PENSEROSO

WITH THE PAINTINGS BY
WILLIAM BLAKE

TOGETHER WITH
A NOTE UPON THE PAINTINGS BY
CHAUNCEY BREWSTER TINKER

NEW YORK
THE LIMITED EDITIONS CLUB
1954

CONTENTS

A NOTE UPON THE PAINTINGS

THE Pierpont Morgan Library has recently, through the generosity of its newly formed group of Fellows, come into possession of William Blake's twelve illustrations in watercolor for Milton's two "minor poems," *L'Allegro* and *Il Penseroso*. Although these were never engraved or reproduced in any way by the artist, they have long been known to exist, and indeed have been used as illustrations (in collotype) in the Nonesuch edition of Milton's English poems, enriched with notes by Mr. Geoffrey Keynes. The full series, six drawings for *L'Allegro* and six for *Il Penseroso*, was first reproduced in color by Mr. Adrian Van Sinderen in his *Blake, the Mystic Genius*.

The watercolors were accompanied, apparently from the beginning, by twelve sheets of writing in Blake's hand, carrying the lines from the poem which the artist has illustrated, together with some notes mentioning details which are to be found in the pictures. These, too, have been seen and used before, with the exception of the original titles which Blake

7

gave to the pictures. The titles, hitherto overlooked and replaced by others less accurate, are on the verso of the sheets, and have now been found and deciphered as follows: for *L'Allegro: Mirth; The Lark; The Sun at His Eastern Gate; A Sunshine Holiday; The Goblin; The Youthful Poet's Dream;* for *Il Penseroso: Melancholy; The Wandering Moon; The Spirit of Plato; The Sun in His Wrath; Mysterious Dream; Milton, Old Age.* These titles are simpler and somewhat more natural than those devised by W. M. Rossetti, and used by succeeding critics.

The watercolors are on sheets measuring about 6⅜ by 4⅞ inches, and each is signed *W. Blake inv.* The watermark "M & J Lay 1816" is found in the paper on which the designs are painted, and seems therefore to fix a date subsequent to which the watercolors were made. The artist was perhaps entering upon the period of his great labors which were to result in the illustrations for the *Book of Job,* for *Paradise Lost* and for Dante's *Divine Comedy.*

Milton's *L'Allegro* and *Il Penseroso* are two contrasted and highly personal *études* to which he gave two rather inaccurate Italian titles. Blake gave them the still more confusing titles *Mirth* and *Melancholy*. The scenes of the first six are not in every case mirthful, and the lovely figure of *Melancholy* never suggests gloom or depression, or any other mood commonly associated with that word.

Blake's twelve illustrations, though wanting the grotesqueness and sublimity associated with his name, are found on examination to have a strangeness and an esoteric quality quite their own. Indeed students and interpreters of the symbols used by Blake—by no means always in agreement with one another—will have much to say about the tiny details which fill to overflowing the scenes set before us. The drawings are of course never merely illustrative of what the artist found in the brief and flashing scenes of the two companion poems. Here, as elsewhere, he uses the poems to enable him to give expression to his own philosophy of existence, and to his somewhat novel view of the relation of the sexes. But though he departs often enough from the spirit of his Miltonic originals he does not pass by the gaiety of the two opening pictures of the *Allegro* group or the deepening sense of solemnity as the whole series progresses. These aspects of Blake's work can be and should be enjoyed by those who feel a natural delight in the man's vivid and blending colors and in the dreamlike scenes which he has the power to call up before us.

One aspect of Blake's world of the imagination as seen by the ordinary observer like myself may perhaps be described.

9

It is a kind of freedom from stifling material conditions. As the twelve watercolors are examined in turn, we never have the sense of being "shut in," whether in the gaiety of the Elizabethan theatre of *L'Allegro* or the "studious cloister's pale" of *Il Penseroso*. We have an abiding sense of being in the open—almost, one might say, *"en plein air,"* if it were not that our sight is extended beyond our mortal ken. The human beings, no less than the (more important) fairies, spirits, emanations and allegorical figures that fill the scene, are not restricted by the "ordinary" boundaries of life or limited by laws falsely considered natural.

The artist's first interest is not in human beings, their pastoral occupations and humble pleasures. Milton speaks of Corydon and Thyrsis as "at their savoury dinner set Of herbs and other country messes, Which the neat-handed Phillis dresses"; Blake mentions them also, but reduces all such creatures—the laboring ploughman, the merry milkmaid, and even woods and trees—to "small figures," as he phrases it. They are indeed all but invisible, as may be shown from his third picture in the *Allegro* series, *The Sun at His Eastern Gate*. It is the life-giving and imperial god that delights the painter, because he is a potent force, arising in splendor, attended by his suitors, clouds "in their liveries," with hosts of winged beings,

10

ministering spirits, no doubt, bringers of good things to men at dawn. Beauteous is the princely Sun at his appearing, but dire is his smiting wrath at noonday.

Again, in *The Goblin* drawing, we have the same impression of conditions transcended. There is, to be sure, a bedroom visible, with fairies dancing on the floor, the coverlet of the bed and, astonishingly, on the ceiling, while a ghost (Blake assures us that it is a ghost) stands at the foot of the bed, tormenting the poor occupant.

But all this is only a *glimpse*. What is going on in the air around is more important. Say what you may of details, it is the Goblin who fills the scene. In the *poem* the fiend, after his kindly miracle, is described as "stretched out all the chimney's length," basking in front of the fire, his labors ended. Thus Milton suggests a pleasant interior scene, somewhat in the Dutch manner; but Blake will have none of it. The stupendous Goblin, yawning and stretching with weariness, drops the flail with which he has done his work and the cream-bowl which was his reward, and begins his disappearance into thin air. Far above in the sky, Fairy Mab is shown eating the junkets. On earth some belated traveler follows "the Friar's Lantern towards the Convent." Plainly there is mischief abroad, and the Powers of the Air are astir.

The last picture in the *Allegro* group is, appropriately, *The Youthful Poet's Dream*, which Blake apparently regards as the climax of his work thus far. The boy Milton slumbers upon a bank under a tree; beside him there is a large unwritten folio volume, while his right hand holds a pen and his left is slightly raised as though responsive, even in sleep, to the dream above his head. The sun, which has been shown before in his glory, is now sinking, and the flowing stream and the cool air are already haunted by fairylike beings. But there is a greater and a supreme Power at work upon the youthful poet—the "Sun of Imagination" which dwarfs the setting sun, large as that is, and which appears as a vast sphere above the dreamer's head while Shakespeare and Ben Jonson, as the masters of masque and antique pageantry, preside over it, on either hand. And here there enters the series the theme of Hymen ("with saffron robe and taper clear") which, even if one fully understood it, could hardly be translated into words. Let the reader instruct himself by searching out the number of embracing lovers which may be found here and elsewhere in the series. To follow the artist's lead in such a way is more remunerative than the scrupulous acceptance of commentators' explanations.

Melancholy is, as I have said, erroneously named, for her sweet and solemn figure is attended by the maidens "Peace" and "Quiet," and "Leisure," the lover of trim gardens. To the right and left of her head are the silent figure of "Night," soothed by the nightingale's song, and the "New Moon" checking her dragon-team above the oak. *Melancholy* is, in truth, none other than "Wisdom's best Nurse," "Contemplation." Beside her is "Spare Fast" (apt personification of a poet!), who lifts his eyes to a vision of the circling Muses above his head, even as she herself raises her own to the flaming cherub who guides the fiery wheels of the Throne of God. In color, composition and lucidity, this is certainly among the loveliest of the pictures.

As Milton's preference was for *Il Penseroso*, so, I think, was Blake's. In the last five of the drawings he introduces Milton himself as a principal figure; and in one of them (the second, or *The Wandering Moon*) he attempts to depict the same setting that Milton uses when listening to the sullen toll of the curfew, borne across some wide-watered shore—a passage reminiscent of the *squilla di lontano* in Dante's *Purgatorio* (canto VIII).

But here we must not go astray. Blake was never greatly interested in pure landscape. He paints no soft nocturne. He does, it is true, give us a pleasant glimpse of the wide-watered shore, with a church-tower in the middle distance, and the Moon high in heaven. But Cynthia is no serene goddess, only

13

a short-skirted fay, who appears directly before the eyes of John Milton, student at Christ's College, Cambridge, in long robe and mortarboard with pompon. This is hardly Romanticism. Here is no solemn ode to Evening. Blake's moon is vivid enough, and behind her are the radiant emblems by which she is known; but Blake has made it difficult to think of her as wandering disconsolate along heaven's pathless way, for we do not easily detect any trace of terror about her. We must re-read the artist's picture until we find the meaning which he tells us is there.

Milton's studies at Cambridge are shown us in the next drawing, entitled *The Spirit of Plato*. Here the young student, meditating upon an open volume, is confronted by the shade of the great Greek philosopher, and the Platonic heaven (according to Blake) is opened before him in a splendid confusion of classical detail which the artist has spared no pains in elaborating. The four Elements; the three Destinies; and the spheres of Venus, Mars and Jupiter are revealed in a vast scene of light, color line and symbol.

"Melancholy" has of course no part in this scene, and, in fact, appears but once again in the series, when, in the fourth picture, she leads the poet through the fierce shafts of the Sun in his mid-day wrath towards the cool shades of a quiet grove.

As the two of them pass along their way, Blake bids us notice that the trees are under the domination of insects raised by the Sun's heat—a surprising contrast to the majesty of The *Sun at His Eastern Gate*.

This domination, however, does not extend to the scene depicted in the fifth watercolor, where the dream-imagery is again employed. The poet slumbering upon the ground is surrounded by six small fairylike figures "hovering on the air" with instruments of music. Here the *dominant* figure is the personification of "Sleep" (or rather of the inspiration conveyed in sleep)—a vast spirit descending from heaven, with the "strange, mysterious dream" upon his enormous pinions. The mystery of course must remain a mystery still; but Blake speaks of it as a process of unveiling, with "Scrolls and Nets and Webs, unfolded by Spirits in the Air and in the Brook." The sweep and the splendor of this conception of divine inspiration, personified and visible before us, are a fine example of Blake's transcendent genius.

In the final scene of all, Milton is represented as in old age. Seated in his "mossy cell," with open book and lighted lamp, he is still lost in contemplation of the heavens, whence power had descended long since upon him. There is no hint of blindness, which Blake apparently refuses to recognize. Whether the poet rightly "spells" the constellations over his head is a matter of no great importance. Above belted Orion, with lifted sword, we behold four signs of the zodiac, the Ram, the Bull, Gemini and the Crab, which must be taken to indicate spring and early summer; for on earth all is bursting into life. At the poet's side the rose and the lily take visible human form, and the whole of nature is "commercing with the skies." The poet's arms are opened wide in rapt wonder at the glory of the universe, and his lips are parted as he breaks into prophetic song.

IL PENSEROSO

BY

JOHN MILTON
&
WILLIAM BLAKE

IL PENSEROSO

Hence vain deluding Joys,

   The brood of Folly without father bred!

How little you bestead,

   Or fill the fixèd mind with all your toys;

Dwell in some idle brain,

   And fancies fond with gaudy shapes possess,

As thick and numberless

   As the gay motes that people the sun-beams,

Or likest hovering dreams

   The fickle Pensioners of Morpheus' train.

But hail, thou Goddess, sage and holy,

Hail, divinest Melancholy!

Whose Saintly visage is too bright

To hit the sense of human sight;

And therefore to our weaker view,

O'er-laid with black, staid Wisdom's hue.

Black, but such as in esteem,

Prince Memnon's sister might beseem,

Or that Starred Ethiope Queen that strove

To set her beauty's praise above

The Sea Nymphs, and their powers offended.

Yet thou art higher far descended

Thee bright-haired Vesta long of yore,

MILTON'S VISION OF THE MOON

To solitary Saturn bore;

His daughter she (in Saturn's reign,

Such mixture was not held a stain).

Oft in glimmering Bowers, and glades

He met her, and in secret shades

Of woody Ida's inmost grove,

Whilst yet there was no fear of Jove.

Come, pensive Nun, devout and pure,

Sober, steadfast, and demure,

All in a robe of darkest grain,

Flowing with majestic train,

And sable stole of Cypress Lawn,

Over thy decent shoulders drawn.

Come, but keep thy wonted state,

With even step, and musing gait,

And looks commercing with the skies,

Thy rapt soul sitting in thine eyes:

There, held in holy passion still,

Forget thy self to Marble, till

With a sad Leaden downward cast,

Thou fix them on the earth as fast.

And join with thee calm Peace, and Quiet,

Spare Fast, that oft with gods doth diet,

And hears the Muses in a ring,

Aye round about Jove's Altar sing.

And add to these retired Leisure,

MILTON AND THE SPIRIT OF PLATO

That in trim Gardens takes his pleasure;

But first, and chiefest, with thee bring,

Him that yon soars on golden wing,

Guiding the fiery-wheeled throne,

The Cherub Contemplation,

And the mute Silence hist along,

'Less Philomel will deign a Song,

In her sweetest, saddest plight,

Smoothing the rugged brow of Night,

While Cynthia checks her Dragon yoke,

Gently o'er th' accustomed Oak;

Sweet Bird, that shunn'st the noise of folly,

Most musical, most melancholy!

Thee, Chauntress, oft the Woods among,

I woo to hear thy even-song;

And missing thee, I walk unseen

On the dry smooth-shaven Green,

To behold the wandering Moon,

Riding near her highest noon,

Like one that had been led astray

Through the Heaven's wide pathless way;

And oft, as if her head she bowed,

Stooping through a fleecy cloud.

Oft on a Plat of rising ground,

I hear the far-off Curfew sound,

Over some wide-watered shore,

MILTON LED BY MELANCHOLY

Swinging slow with sullen roar;

Or if the Air will not permit,

Some still removèd place will fit,

Where glowing Embers through the room

Teach light to counterfeit a gloom,

Far from all resort of mirth,

Save the Cricket on the hearth,

Or the Bellman's drowsy charm,

To bless the doors from nightly harm

Or let my Lamp, at midnight hour,

Be seen in some high lonely Tower,

Where I may oft out-watch the Bear,

With thrice great Hermes, or unsphere

The spirit of Plato to unfold

What Worlds, or what vast Regions hold

The immortal mind that hath forsook

Her mansion in this fleshly nook

And of those Daemons that are found

In fire, air, flood, or under ground,

Whose power hath a true consent

With Planet, or with Element.

Some time let Gorgeous Tragedy

In Sceptered Pall come sweeping by,

Presenting Thebes, or Pelops' line,

Or the tale of Troy divine,

Or what (though rare) of later age,

MILTON'S DREAM

Ennoblèd hath the Buskined stage.

   But, O sad Virgin, that thy power

Might raise Musaeus from his bower,

Or bid the soul of Orpheus sing

Such notes as, warbled to the string,

Drew Iron tears down Pluto's cheek,

And made Hell grant what Love did seek.

Or call up him that left half told

The story of Cambuscan bold,

Of Camball, and of Algarsife,

And who had Canace to wife,

That owned the virtuous Ring and Glass,

And of the wondrous Horse of Brass,

On which the Tartar King did ride;

And if aught else great Bards beside,

In sage and solemn tunes have sung,

Of Tourneys and of Trophies hung;

Of Forest, and enchantments drear,

Where more is meant than meets the ear.

Thus, Night, oft see me in thy pale career,

Till civil-suited Morn appear,

Not tricked and frounced as she was wont,

With the Attic Boy to hunt,

But Kerchiefed in a comely Cloud,

While rocking Winds are Piping loud,

Or ushered with a shower still,

THE PEACEFUL HERMITAGE

When the gust hath blown his fill,

Ending on the rustling Leaves,

With minute-drops from off the Eaves.

And when the Sun begins to fling

His flaring beams, me, Goddess, bring

To archèd walks of twilight groves,

And shadows brown, that Sylvan loves,

Of Pine, or monumental Oak,

Where the rude Ax with heavèd stroke,

Was never heard the Nymphs to daunt,

Or fright them from their hallowed haunt.

There in close covert by some Brook,

Where no profaner eye may look,

Hide me from Day's garish eye,

While the Bee with Honied thigh,

That at her flowery work doth sing,

And the Waters murmuring

With such consort as they keep,

Entice the dewy-feathered Sleep;

And let some strange mysterious dream,

Wave at his Wings, in Airy stream

Of lively portraiture displayed,

Softly on my eye-lids laid.

And as I wake, sweet music breathe

Above, about, or underneath,

Sent by some Spirit to mortals good,

Or th' unseen Genius of the Wood.

  But let my due feet never fail,

To walk the studious Cloister's pale,

And love the high embowèd Roof,

With antique Pillars massy proof.

And storied Windows richly dight,

Casting a dim religious light.

There let the pealing Organ blow,

To the full voiced choir below,

In Service high, and Anthems clear,

As may with sweetness, through mine ear,

Dissolve me into ecstasies,

And bring all Heaven before mine eyes.

And may at last my weary age

Find out the peaceful hermitage,

The Hairy Gown and Mossy Cell,

Where I may sit and rightly spell

Of every Star that Heaven doth shew,

And every Herb that sips the dew;

Till old experience do attain

To something like Prophetic strain.

These pleasures, Melancholy, give,

And I with thee will choose to live.

BLAKE'S INSCRIPTIONS ON HIS PAINTINGS

MELANCHOLY AND HER COMPANIONS

These personifications are all brought together in this design, surrounding the Principal Figure Who is Melancholy Herself.

MILTON'S VISION OF THE MOON

Milton in his character of a Student at Cambridge, sees the Moon terrified as one led astray in the midst of her path thru heaven. The distant Steeple seen across a wide water indicates the sound of the Curfew Bell.

MILTON AND THE SPIRIT OF PLATO

The Spirit of Plato unfolds his Worlds to Milton in Contemplation. The Three Destinies sit on the Circles of Plato's Heavens, weaving the Thread of Mortal Life; these Heavens are Venus, Jupiter & Mars. Hermes flies before as attending on the Heaven of Jupiter; the Great Bear is seen in the sky beneath Hermes & the Spirits of Fire, Air, Water & Earth Surround Milton's Chair.

MILTON LED BY MELANCHOLY

Milton led by Melancholy into the Groves away from the Sun's flaming Beams, who is seen in the Heavens throwing his darts & flames of fire. The Spirits of the Trees on each side are seen under the domination of Insects raised by the Sun's heat.

MILTON'S DREAM

Milton Sleeping on a Bank; Sleep descending, with a strange, Mysterious dream upon his Wings, of Scrolls & Nets & Webs, unfolded by Spirits in the Air & in the Brook. Around Milton are Six Spirits or Fairies, hovering on the air, with Instruments of Music.

THE PEACEFUL HERMITAGE

Milton in his Old Age sitting in his "Mossy Cell," Contemplating the Constellations, surrounded by the Spirits of the Herbs & Flowers, bursts forth into a rapturous Prophetic Strain.

Of this volume, in which John Milton's two poems are printed dos-à-dos, seventeen hundred and eighty copies have been made, of which number fifteen hundred copies are reserved for the members of The Limited Editions Club and two hundred eighty are reserved for the Fellows of The Pierpont Morgan Library. The illustrations of William Blake have been reproduced from the original drawings now in the possession of The Pierpont Morgan Library, by special permission of the Library's Trustees. The text has been composed in Jan Van Krimpen's Van Dyck types by Mackenzie & Harris in San Francisco, and printed by The Thistle Press in New York; the reproductions have been made as gravures by the Photogravure & Color Company; and the whole work has been planned by Bruce Rogers.

This is copy number **1013**

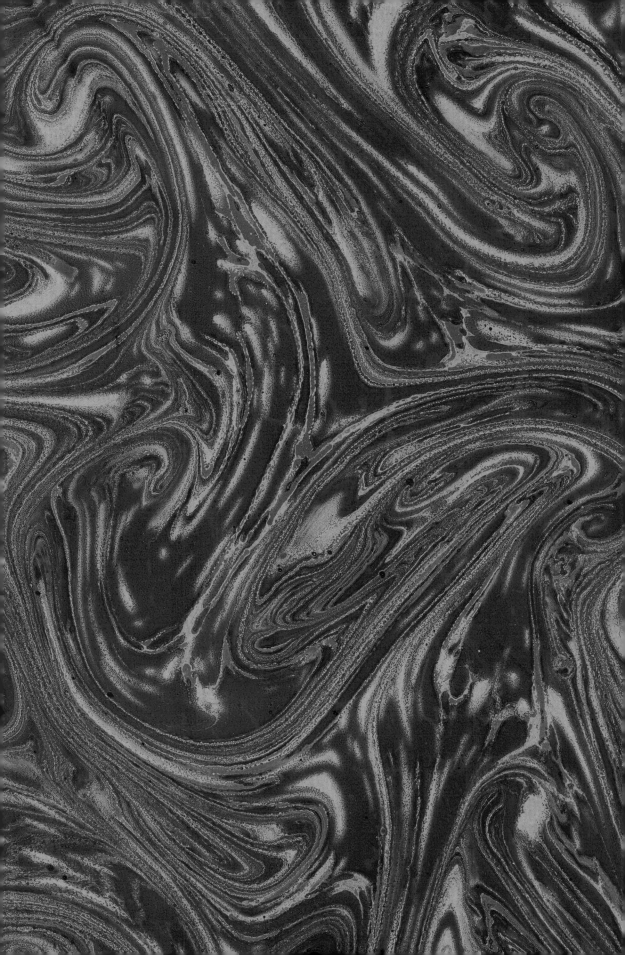